2796 d. 295

ROBERT BURNS'

COMMON PLACE BOOK.

Printed from the Original Manuscript

IN THE POSSESSION OF JOHN ADAM, ESQ.,
GREENOCK.

EDINBURGH.
𝔓𝔯𝔦𝔳𝔞𝔱𝔢𝔩𝔶 𝔓𝔯𝔦𝔫𝔱𝔢𝔡.

1 8 7 2.

PREFACE.

THE *Original Manuscript Commonplace-Book* of ROBERT BURNS, is here given to the public in its entire and primitive shape for the first time. Only *now* can it be said, the *Book* is given as Burns wrote it, *from day to day*, in those, his early days, when, as yet, the world had never heard of him. Editions of "BURNS" are as the sands of the sea for multitude; many of great excellence, stored with fresh and original matter, contain notices of the Commonplace-Book and versions, more or less connected, of portions of its contents, yet, strange to say, no ONE edition has it, in its first shape, in its original connection, and in its full extent. These extracts, merely copied by one Editor from another, can here at *last* be referred to the *original* of all the copies : and it will be abundantly plain that no one of the Editors, from Currie, down to the latest, had access to the *genuine original Manuscript*.

Burns evidently sent an *amended* and interpolated *copy* of the MS. to *Captain Riddel* (to whom he addressed the " Observations on Scottish Song") prefaced with the following :—

"On rummaging over some old papers I lighted on a MS. of my early years, in which I had determined to write myself out; as I was placed by fortune among a class of men to whom my ideas would have been nonsense, I had meant that the book should have lain by me, in the fond hope, that some time or other, even after I was no more, my thoughts would fall into the hands of somebody capable of appreciating their value." And this is the source of all the versions, copied by each successive editor, carefully adhered to by all, the touched "*Replica*," NOT the original picture, as can be seen on collation of the already printed portions, with any page of this reproduction of the original. In a London dealer's catalogue, a few years ago, appeared the sale notice among some Burnsiana, of "*Burns' Commonplace-Book begun in April* 1783.—*Observations, Hints, Songs, Scraps of Poetry, by Robert Burness, a man who had little art in making money and still less in keeping it.*" Among the Contents, are cited—"*O once I loved a bonnie lass*" —"*Criticism,*"—"*Remorse,*"—"*Penitential Thought,*"— "*Observations on the Vice of Human Nature,*"—"*O thou great Being,*"—"*The Wintry West,*"—"*My Father was a Farmer,*"—Observations on writing Love verses,— "*Behind yon hills where Stincher flows.*" *Epitaphs (two unprinted),*—"*Observations on the species of men,*"— (the original sketch of) "*Green grows the rashes, O,*"— "*Prayer,*"—"*Despondency,*"—"*Tibby I hae seen the day,*" —(early song not printed) "*My girl is airy, she's buxom and gay,"—" John Barley Corn, a song to its own tune,"* (curious note),—" 1*st Epistle to Lapraik,"* with the date 1st April, 1785, (superior readings to Currie's),—"*On receiving an answer to the above I wrote the following, April* 21*st, 1785* ;" then follows the 2d Epistle, "*Man was made to mourn,"* reflections on his fate,—"*When first 1 came to Stewart Kyle,"* fragment not printed, and "*Now breezy Win's and slaughtering Guns,"* the four last lines of which are

> Now waving crops, with yellow tops,
> Delight the weary *Farmer,*
> An' the moon shines bright when I rove at night
> To muse on *Jeanie Armour.*

The name in the last line expressed in short hand. Notes on old Scots Songs, &c. The MS. now published : found to be as described, and in the most perfect condition : 11 sheets, 16 ins. by 12½, broached with a coarse thread, the outward figure of the book so rude and common, that, on looking at it, one feels an overwhelming conviction that it is *now* in the form, with the leaves in the precise position they occupied when Burns bought the blank paper and had it stitched for him, most likely, in "wee Jonnie Wilson's Shop," in Kilmarnock. The watermarks on the paper—right, a group of figures, motto, *Pro Patria ;* left, circular, doubled intertwined cyphers *E.B.,* give the curious a clue to date and maker. Page 1, elaborately careful, evidently Burns' handwriting, but of juvenile cast, with its double motto from Shenstone, was plainly written long before any of the "*Observations*" had connected existence, at least on paper. Page 2, blank. Pp. 3 to 42, written on both sides of the sheets with *paging,* "*catchwords,*" and marginal dates, all in Burns' handwriting. P. 43, (unpaged) about one-third occupied by writing. Page 44, entirely blank. The writing is bold, clear, perfectly decipherable in every part, full of spirit and character, the letter forms peculiar and striking, seem to grow in size with the intensity of the sentiment, in such phrases as the "*Lash of Remorse*" assume weird and gigantic forms bodying forth to the eye the horrors of the mind, as if that lash had not simply *nine* but 999 tails; but then "*My Nannie, O,*" is registered in letters as big, and the often named master-passion always appears recorded in letters of a size suiting its high position and estimation in the Poet's breast. The corrections, substitutions, interlineations, and variations are most curious and deeply interesting throughout: on page 3d, at line 6th, some daring hand has ventured a correction, and deleting *one* word of Burns', has inserted *three* of somebody else's, converting the phrase "*Green Eighteen*" into "*a Youth of Eighteen.*" This is a solitary instance, there is scarcely a blot, and not *one erasure* from end to end of the MS. Beginning with the date, April 1783, and ending with October 1785— here appear in their first, unvarnished shape, long before they were prepared for the public eye, the two Epistles to " *Lapraik*,"—" *Man was made to mourn*,"—" *Green grows the Rashes, O,*"—" *John Barleycorn*,"—" *Death and dying words of poor Maillie,*" and many other less important pieces. At the date "*April* '83," we notice the germ of a beautiful stanza of the " Cottar's Saturday Night," the variants of omission, insertion, and alteration from the printed copies, give us a glance into the Poet's workshop, enabling us to judge of the value of his *revise*, and of the quality of his work, by the first state of his thoughts, in the rough.

The reproduction of the Original has been made with the most scrupulous adherence to the exact form in which it exists, in the most minute particulars, the orthography has been preserved in every instance, the punctuation retained, wherever any indication of it existed, no single word has been added, no one altered, or omitted and with the most perfect truth, it may be said that *this*, the most interesting record of the first phase of the literary career of Burns, is given absolutely as he left it. Here it is that Burns' genius receives its first illustration, the dawnings of the day of Song here first struggle above the horizon, the first uncertain pipings of his muse find a bashful utterance, and all as yet unknown, uncared for, by the circle of his neighbours and fellow-rustics, as by the greater world outside, he rules his little inner realm of thought and fancy; deals praise and blame, now pauses over some pleasant or painful fancy, and now blazes forth in all the fire and vigour of the creative Poet's highest mood.   The forms of things bodied forth may to some provoke a smile, but to the earnest mind, answering to the touch of Reverence, there is a something awe striking in thus, as it were, looking over the shoulder of the greatest lyrical Poet our country has produced, wrestling with his genius in its very birth-pangs: food for contemplation in watching the first emergence in these unstudied efforts, of poetic thoughts that *now*, glittering of surface, blazing with colour, and fair of form, have won a place of honour among the choicest jewels of the Classic Literature of our country.   The world of care and pains bestowed by the Poet in perfecting the form of his thought can only be guessed by a close perusal of this MS. collated with the printed copies.

Manuscript notes in, at least, two different hands occur on the MS. at different places.   Those initialed " *J.S.* " are the most important, and would seem to have been done at Burns' request to guide him in a selection for his then projected *first edition*, printed late in 1786, about twelve months after the close of the MS.   J. S. are the initials, it is probable, of Burns' close friend *James Smith*, to whom the poetic epistle "Dear Smith, the sleest pawkie thief," was addressed, a shopkeeper in Mauchline, during Burns' Ayrshire period.   In 1788, a calico printer at Avon, near Linlithgow, as we find by a letter of Burns' to him, of date April in that year, informing him of his (Burns') marriage to " a certain clean-limbed, handsome, bewitching hussy," ordering one

of Smith's best shawls, as he desired that the work of
one whose friendship he counted on as a life-rent lease,
should be the first present he made to his bride. Smith
emigrated to the West Indies some years later, where he
died not long after. Of a ready wit and lively manners
he was much respected by the Poet, and the markings
on the MS. are proofs that he was so.

The contents of the MS. are beyond the *reach*, as they
are beyond the need of criticism. The present posses-
sor, Mr John Adam, Town-Chamberlain of Greenock,
has permitted the publication, as a tribute of reverence
to the memory of Burns, and with the design of pre-
serving authentic *copies*, should any unforeseen accident
befall the *Original*.

C. D. L.

GREENOCK, *January 25th*, 1872.

Observations, Hints, Songs, Scraps of Poetry, &c.,
by Robt. Burness; a man who had little art in making
money, and still less in keeping it; but was, however, a
man of some sense, a great deal of honesty, and unbounded
good-will to every creature—rational or irrational. As
he was but little indebted to scholastic education, and
bred at a plough-tail, his performances must be strongly
tinctured with his unpolished, rustic way of life; but, as
I believe they are really HIS OWN, it may be some enter-
tainment to a curious observer of human-nature to see
how a ploughman thinks and feels under the pressure
of Love, Ambition, Anxiety, Grief, with the like cares
and passions, which, however diversified by the modes
and manners of life, operate pretty much alike, I believe,
in all the Species.

A

"There are numbers in the world who do not want
"sense to make a figure, so much as an opinion of their
"own abilities, to put them upon recording their observa-
"tions, and allowing them the same importance which
"they do to those which appear in print."—SHENSTONE.

"Pleasing when youth is long expir'd to trace,
"The forms our pencil, or our pen design'd.
"Such was our youthful air, and shape, and face!
"Such the soft image of our youthful mind."

IBIDEM.

1783. 24 years of age. April —83. Notwithstanding all that has been said against Love, respecting the folly and weakness it leads a young unexperienced mind into; still I think it, in a great measure, deserves the highest encomiums that have been passed upon it. If any thing on earth deserves the name of rapture or transport, it is the feelings of green eighteen in the company of the mistress of his heart when she repays him with an equal return of affection.

Aug. There is certainly some connection between Love, Music, and Poetry; and therefore, I have always thought it a fine touch of Nature, that passage in a modern love composition:

> " As towards her cot he jogg'd along
> " Her name was frequent in his song."

For my own part I never had the least thought or inclination of turning Poet till I got once heartily in Love, and then Rhyme and Song were, in a manner, the spontaneous language of my heart. The following composition was the first of my performances, and done at an early period of life, when my heart glowed with honest warm simplicity; unacquainted, and uncorrupted with the ways of a wicked world. The performance is, indeed, very puerile and silly: but I am always pleased with it, as it recals to my mind those happy

days when my heart was yet honest, and my tongue
was sincere. The subject of it was a young girl
who really deserved all the praises I have bestowed
on her. I not only had this opinion of Her then—
but I actually think so still, now that the spell is long
since broken, and the inchantment at an end.

SONG.

Tune—I am a man unmarried.

I.

O once I lov'd a bonny lass
    Ay, and I love her still
And whilst that virtue warms my breast
    I'll love my handsome Nell
            Fal lal de lal &c.

2.

As bonny lasses I hae seen,
    And mony full as braw;
But for a modest gracefu' mien,
    The like I never saw.

3.

A bonny lass I will confess
    Is pleasant to the e'e;
But without some better qualities
    She's no a lass for me.

4.

But Nelly's looks are blythe and sweet,
　And what is best of a',
Her reputation is compleat
　And fair without a flaw.

5.

She dresses ay sae clean and neat,
　Both decent and genteel ;
And then there's something in her gate
　Gars ony dress look weel.

6.

A gaudy dress and gentle air
　May slightly touch the heart ;
But it's innocence and modesty
　That polishes the dart.

7.

'Tis this in Nelly pleases me ;
　'Tis this inchants my soul ;
For absolutely in my breast
　She reigns without controul.

FINIS.

CRITICISM ON THE FOREGOING SONG.

Lest my works should be thought below criticism; or meet with a critic who, perhaps, will not look on them with so candid and favourable an eye; I am determined to criticise them myself.

The first distic of the first stanza is quite too much in the flimsy strain of our ordinary street ballads; and on the other hand, the second distic is too much in the other extreme. The expression is a little awkward, and the sentiment too serious. Stanza the second I am well pleased with; and I think it conveys a fine idea of that amiable part of the Sex—the agreeables; or what in our Scotch dialect we call a sweet sonsy Lass. The third stanza has a little of the flimsy turn in it; and the third line has rather too serious a cast. The fourth stanza is a very indifferent one; the first line is, indeed, all in the strain of the second stanza, but the rest is mostly an expletive. The thoughts in the fifth stanza come finely up to my favourite idea of a sweet sonsy Lass; the last line, however, halts a little. The same sentiments are kept up with equal spirit and tenderness in the sixth stanza, but the second and fourth lines, ending with short syllables, hurts the whole. The seventh stanza has several minute faults; but I remember I composed it in a wild enthusiasm of passion, and to this hour I never recollect it, but my heart melts, and my blood sallies at the remembrance.

Sept. I entirely agree with that judicious philosopher Mr Smith in his excellent Theory of Moral Sentiments, that Remorse is the most painful sentiment that can embitter the human bosom. Any ordinary pitch of fortitude may bear up tolerably well, under those calamities, in the procurement of which, we ourselves have had no hand; but when our own follies or crimes have made us miserable and wretched, to bear it up with manly firmness, and at the same time have a proper penitential sense of our misconduct,—is a glorious effort of self-command.

Of all the numerous ills that hurt our peace;
That press the soul, or wring the mind with anguish;
Beyond comparison the worst are those
By our own folly, or our guilt brought on.
In ev'ry other circumstance the mind
Has this to say, it was no deed of mine:
But, when to all the evil of misfortune
This sting is added, blame thy foolish self;
Or worser far, the pangs of keen remorse:
The tort'ring, gnawing consciousness of guilt—
Of guilt, perhaps, where we've involved others;
The young, the innocent, who fondly lov'd us;
Nay more, that very love their cause of ruin.
O! burning hell in all thy store of torments
There's not a keener Lash.
Lives there a man so firm who, while his heart
Feels all the bitter horrors of his crime,

Can reason down it's agonizing throbs,
And, after proper purpose of amendment,
Can firmly force his jarring thoughts to peace.
O happy, happy, enviable man!
O glorious magnanimity of soul!

March, '84. A penitential thought in the hour of Remorse,
            Intended for a tragedy.

All devil as I am—a damned wretch—
A hardened, stubborn, unrepenting villain;
Still my heart melts at human wretchedness;
And with sincere, though unavailing sighs
I view the helpless children of distress.
With tears indignant I behold th' Oppressor
Rejoicing in the honest man's destruction
Whose unsubmitting heart was all his crime.
Even you, ye hapless crew, I pity you,
Ye, whom the seeming good think sin to pity:
Ye, poor, despis'd, abandoned vagabonds
Whom vice as usual, has turned o'er to ruin.
O but for kind, though ill requited friends
I had been driven forth like you forlorn
The most detested, worthless wretch among ye!
O! injured God! thy goodness has endow'd me
With talents passing most of my compeers,
Which I in just proportion have abus'd

As far surpassing other common villains
As Thou in nat'ral parts hast given me more.

I have often observed in the course of my experience of human life that every man, even the worst, have something good about them, though very often nothing else than a happy temperament of constitution inclining them to this or that virtue; on this likewise depend a great many, no man can say how many, of our vices; for this reason no man can say in what degree any person besides himself can be, with strict justice, called wicked. Let any of the strictest character for regularity of conduct among us, examine impartially how many of his virtues are owing to constitution and education; how many vices he has never been guilty of, not from any care or vigilance, but from want of opportunity, or some accidental circumstance intervening; how many of the weaknesses of mankind he has escaped because he was out of the line of such temptation; and what often, if not always, weighs more than all the rest; how much he is indebted to the world's good, because the world does not know all; I say, any man who can thus think, will scan the failings, nay the faults and crimes of mankind around him, with a brother's eye.

March, '84. I have often coveted the acquaintance of that part of mankind commonly known by the ordinary phrase of blackguards, sometimes farther than was consistent with the safety of my character; those who, by thoughtless prodigality or headstrong passions, have been driven to ruin; though disgraced by follies, nay, sometimes " stained with guilt and crimson'd o'er with crimes," I have yet found among them, in not a few instances, some of the noblest virtues, magnanimity, generosity, disinterested friendship, and even modesty, in the highest perfection.

March, '84. There was a certain period of my life that my spirit was broke by repeated losses and disasters, which threatened and indeed affected the utter ruin of my fortune. My body, too, was attacked by that most dreadful distemper, a hypochondria, or confirmed melancholy; in this · wretched state, the recollection of which makes me yet shudder, I hung my harp on the willow trees, except in some lucid intervals, in one of which I composed the following :—

> O Thou great Being! what Thou art
>   Surpassest me to know;
> Yet sure I am, that known to thee
>   Are all affairs below.
>
> Thy creature here, before thee stands,
>   All wretched and distrest;
> Yet sure those ills that press my soul
>   Obey thy high behest.
>
> Sure Thou All-Perfect canst not act
>   From cruelty, or wrath.

O ! free my weary eyes from tears,
    Or close them fast in death.

But if I must afflicted be
    To suit some wise design ;
O ! man my soul with firm resolves
    To bear and not repine.

FINIS.

April. As I am what the men of the world, if they knew of such a man, would call a whimsical mortal ; I have various sources of pleasure and enjoyment which are, in a manner, peculiar to myself ; or some here and there such other out-of-the-way person. Such is the peculiar pleasure I take in the season of winter, more than the rest of the year. This, I believe, may be partly owing to my misfortunes giving my mind a melancholy cast ; but there is something even in the

" Mighty tempest and the hoary waste
" Abrupt and deep stretch'd o'er the buried earth,"

which raises the mind to a serious sublimity, favourable to every thing great and noble. There is scarcely any earthly object gives me more—I don't know if I should call it pleasure, but something which exalts me, something which enraptures me—than to walk in the sheltered side of a wood or high plantation, in a cloudy, winter day, and hear a stormy wind howling among the trees and

raving o'er the plain.   It is my best season for devotion ;
my mind is rapt up in a kind of enthusiasm to *Him* who,
in the pompous language of Scripture, " walks on the
wings of the wind."   In one of these seasons, just after
a tract of misfortunes, I composed the following

SONG.

Tune—Mc Pherson's Farewel.

I.

The wintry West extends his blast
    And hail and rain does blaw ;
Or the stormy North sends driving forth
    The blinding sleet and snaw ;
And tumbling brown, the burn comes down,
    And roars frae bank to brae ;
And bird and beast in covert rest,
    And pass the weary day.

2.

" The sweeping blast, the sky o'ercast,"
    The joyless winter day ;
Let others fear, to me more dear
    Than all the pride of May.
The tempest's howl it sooths my soul,
    My griefs it seems to join ;
The leafless trees my fancy please,
    Their fate resembles mine.

3.

Thou Power Supreme whose mighty scheme,
    These woes of mine fulfil :
Here firm, I rest, they must (be) best,
    Because they are thy will :
Then all I want—(O do Thou grant
    This one request of mine ;)
Since to enjoy, Thou dost deny,
    Assist me to resign.

FINIS.

April. The following Song is a wild Rhapsody miserably deficient in versification, but as the sentiments are the genuine feelings of my heart, for that reason I have a particular pleasure in conning it over.

SONG.

Tune—The weaver and his shuttle O.

My father was a farmer upon the Carrick border O
And carefully he bred me, in decency and order O
He bade me act a manly part, though I had ne'er a
    farthing O
For without an honest manly heart, no man was worth
    regarding O

Chorus—Row de dow &c.

Then out into the world my course I did determine. O
Tho' to be rich was not my wish, yet to be great was
    charming: O
My talents they were not the worst; nor yet my educa-
    tion; O
Resolv'd was I, at least to try, to mend my situation. ()
In many a way, and vain essay, I courted fortune's
    favour; O
Some cause unseen, still stept between, and frustrate
    each endeavor; O
Some times by foes I was o'erpower'd; sometimes by
    friends forsaken; O
And when my hope was at the top, I still was worst
    mistaken, O
Then sore harass'd and tir'd at last, with fortune's vain
    delusion; O
I dropt my schemes, like idle dreams; and came to this
    conclusion; O
The past was bad, and the future hid; its good or ill
    untryèd; O
But the present hour was in my pow'r and so I would
    enjoy it, O
No help, nor hope, nor view had I; nor person to be-
    friend me; O
So I must toil, and sweat and moil, and labour to sustain
    me, O
To plough and sow, to reap and mow, my father bred
    me early, O

For one, he said, to labor bred, was a match for fortune
    fairly, O
Thus all obscure, unknown, and poor, thro life I'm
    doom'd to wander, O
Till down my weary bones I lay in everlasting slumber; O
No view nor care, but shun whate'er might breed me
    pain or sorrow; O
I live to day as well's I may, regardless of to-morrow, O
But chearful still, I am as well as a monarch in a palace; O
Tho' fortune's frown still hunts me down, with all her
    wonted malice: O
I make, indeed, my daily bread, but ne'er can make it
    farther; O
But as daily bread is all I heed, I do not much regard
    her. O
When sometimes by my labor, I earn a little money, O
Some unforseen misfortune comes generally upon me; O
Mischance, mistake, or by neglect, or my good natur'd
    folly; O
But come what will I've sworn it still, Ill ne'er be
    melancholy. O
All you who follow wealth and power with unremitting
    ardor, O
The more in this you look for bliss, you leave your view
    the further; O
Had you the wealth Potosi boasts, or nations to adore
    you, O
A chearful honest-hearted clown, I will prefer before
    you. O

April. Shenstone observes finely that love-verses writ without any real passion are the most nauseous of all conceits : and I have often thought that no man can be a proper critic of Love composition, except he himself, in one, or more instances, have been a warm votary of this passion. As I have been all along, a miserable dupe to Love, and have been led into a thousand weaknesses and follies by it, for that reason I put the more confidence in my critical skill in distinguishing foppery and conceit, from real passion and nature. Whether the following song will stand the test, I will not pretend to say, because it is my own ; only I can say it was, at the time, real.

SONG.

Tune—As I came in by London O.

Behind yon hills where Stincher flows
'Mong muirs and mosses many, O
The weary sun the day has clos'd
And I'll awa to Nanie. O

CHORUS.

And O my bonny Nannie O,
My young, my handsome Nannie O
Tho' I had the world all at my will,
I would give it all for Nanie. O

The westlin win' blaws loud and shill,
The night's baith dark and rainy O;
But I'll get my plaid and out I'll steal
And o'er the hill to Nanie O.

My Nanie's charming, sweet, and young;
Nae artfu' wiles to win ye O:
May ill befa' the flattering tongue
That would beguile my Nanie O.

Her face is fair, her heart is true,
As spotless as she's bonny O;
The op'ning gowan wet wi dew
Nae purer is than Nanie O.

A country lad is my degree,
And few there be that ken me O,
But what care I how few they be,
I'm welcome ay to Nanie O.

My riches a's my pennie fee,
And I maun guide it canny O,
But warl's gear ne'er troubles me
My thoughts are a' about Nanie O.

Our Guidman delights to view
His sheep and his ky thrive bonny, O
But I'm as blythe that hauds his plew
And haes nae care but Nanie O.

Come weel, come woe, I care na by,
I'll tak what Heaven will sen' me O;
Nae other care in life have I
But live and love my Nanie O.

And O my bonny Nanie O;
My young, my handsome Nanie O
Tho' I had the world all at my will,
I would give it all to Nanie O.

April—Epitaph on Wm. Hood, Senr., in Tarbolton.

Here Souter Hood in death does sleep;
To Hell if he's gane thither,
Satan give him thy gear to keep;
He'll haud it weel the gither.

On Jas. Grieve, Laird of Boghead, Tarbolton.

Here lies Boghead amang the dead,
In hopes to get salvation;
But if such as he, in Heav'n may be,
Then welcome, hail! damnation.

April.—Epitaph on my own friend, and my Father's friend, Wm. Muir in Tarbolton miln.

Here lies a chearful, honest breast,
As e'er God with his image blest.
The friend of man, the friend of Truth;
The friend of age, and guide of youth.
Few hearts like his with virtue warm'd,
Few heads with knowledge so informed.
If there's another world, he lives in bliss;
If there is none, he made the best of this.

April.—Epitaph on my ever honored Father.

O ye! who sympathize with virtue's pains!
Draw near with pious rev'rence and attend;
Here lye the loving Husband's dear remains,
The tender Father, and the generous Friend.
The pitying heart, that felt for human woe,
The dauntless heart, that fear'd no human pride;
The friend of man, to vice alone a foe;
For "even his failings lean'd to virtue's side."

FINIS.

Verse first.—O ye whose hearts deceased merit pains.

April.—I think the whole species of young men may be naturally enough divided in two grand classes, which

I shall call the Grave, and the Merry; tho' by the bye these terms do not with propriety enough express my ideas. There are, indeed, some exceptions; some part of the species who, according to my ideas of these divisions, come under neither of them; such are those individuals whom Nature turns off her hand, oftentimes, very like blockheads, but generally, on a nearer inspection, have somethings surprisingly clever about them. They are more properly men of conceit than men of Genius; men whose heads are filled, and whose faculties are engrossed, by some whimsical notions in some art, or science; so that they cannot think, nor speak with pleasure, on any other subject. Besides this pedantic species, nature has always produced some meer, insipid blockheads, who may be said to live a vegetable life, in this world.

The Grave, I shall cast into the usual division of those who are goaded on; by the love of money; and those whose darling wish, is, to make a figure in the world. The Merry, are the men of pleasure, of all denominations; the jovial lads who have too much fire and spirit to have any settled rule of action; but without much deliberation, follow the strong impulses of nature: the thoughtless; the careless; the indolent; and in particular he who, with a happy sweetness of natural temper, and a cheerful vacancy of thought, steals through life, generally indeed, in poverty and obscurity; but poverty and obscurity are only evils to him who can sit gravely down, and make a repining comparison, between his own situation and that of others; and lastly, to grace the quorum, such are generally the men whose heads are capable of all the towerings of genius, and whose hearts are warmed with the delicacy of feeling.

Aug.—The foregoing was to have been an elaborate dissertation on the various species of men; but as I cannot please myself in the arrangements of my ideas, I must wait till further experience and nicer observation throw more light on the subject. In the mean time I shall set down the following fragment which, as it is the genuine language of my heart, will enable any body to determine which of the classes I belong to.

> Green grow the rashes—O
> Green grow the rashes—O
> The sweetest hours that e'er I spend
> Are spent among the lasses—O.

> There's nought but care on ev'ry hand
> In every hour that passes—O
> What signifies the life o' man
> An' 'twere na for the lasses—O.
> Green grow, &c.
> The warly race may riches chase
> An' riches still may fly them—O

> An' tho' at last they catch them fast
> There hearts can ne'er enjoy them—O.
> > Green grow, &c.
> But gie me a canny hour at e'en
> My arms about my dearie—O
> An' warly cares an' warly men
> May a' goe tapsalteerie—O.
> > Green grow, &c.
> For you that's douse an' sneers at this
> Ye're nought but senseless asses—O
> The wisest man the warl' saw
> He dearly lov'd the lasses, O.

As the grand end of human life is to cultivate an intercourse with that Being to whom we owe life, with ev'ry enjoyment that renders life delightful; and to maintain an integritive conduct towards our fellow creatures; that so by forming piety and virtue into habit, we may be fit members for that society of the pious and the good, which reason and revelation teach us to expect beyond the grave, I do not see that the turn of mind, and pursuits of such a one as the above verses describe—one who spends the hours and thoughts, which the vocations of the day can spare, with Ossian, Shakespeare, Thomson, Shenstone, Sterne, &c. or as the maggot takes him, a gun, a fiddle, or a song to make, or mend; and at all times some hearts-dear bony lass in view—I say I do not see that the turn of mind and pursuits of such a one are in the least more inimical to the sacred interests of Piety and Virtue, than the even lawful, bustling, and straining after the world's riches and honors : and I do not see but he may gain Heaven as well, which by the bye, is no mean consideration, who steals thro' the vale of life, amusing himself with every little flower that fortune throws in his way ; as he who, straining strait forward, and perhaps spattering all about him, gains some of Life's little eminences, where, after all, he can only see and be seen a little more conspicuously, than, what in the pride of his heart, he is apt to term, the poor, indolent, devil he has left behind him.

Aug.—A prayer, when fainting fits, and other alarming symptoms of a pleurisy or some other dangerous disorder, which indeed still threaten me, first put nature on the alarm.

> O Thou Unknown, Almighty Cause
> Of all my hope and fear,
> In whose dread presence ere an hour
> Perhaps I must appear.
>
> If I have wander'd in those paths
> Of life I ought to shun,
> As something loudly in my breast
> Remonstrates I have done.
>
> Thou know'st that Thou hast formed me
> With passions wild and strong ;

And listening to their witching voice
Has often led me wrong.

Where human weakness has come short,
Or frailty stept aside;
Do Thou, All-Good, for such Thou art,
In shades of darkness hide.

Where with intention I have err'd,
No other plea I have,
But Thou art good, and goodness still
Delighteth to forgive.

Aug.—MISGIVINGS IN THE HOUR OF DESPONDENCY AND
PROSPECT OF DEATH.

Why am I loth to leave this earthly scene,
Have I so found it full of pleasing charms?
Some drops of joy with draughts of ill between,
Some gleams of sunshine 'midst renewing storms;
Is it departing pangs my heart alarms
Or Death's unlovely, dreary, dark abode?
For guilt—for guilt my terrors are in arms,
I tremble to approach an angry God
And justly smart beneath his sin-avenging rod.
Fain would I say forgive my foul offence,
Forgive where I so oft have gone astray;
But should my author health again dispence

Again I would desert fair Virtue's way;
Again to passions I would fall a prey,
Again exalt the brute and sink the man,
Then how can I for heavenly mercy pray
Who act so counter Heavenly mercy's plan,
Who sin so oft have mourn'd then to temptation ran.
O Thou great Governor of all below!
If one so black with crimes dare call on Thee;
Thy breath can make the tempest cease to blow,
And still the tumult of the raging sea;
With that controuling Power assist even me
Those headlong, furious passions to confine,
For all unfit my native powers be
To rule their torrent in the allowed line;
O aid me with thy help, omnipotence Divine!

Sept.   SONG.

Tune.—Invercaulds Reel—Strathspey.

CHORUS.

Tibby I hae seen the day
Ye wadna been sae shy
An' for laik o' gear ye lightly me—
    But fien' a hair care I.

Yestreen I met you on the moor
Ye spak na but gaed by like stoor

Ye lightly me because I'm poor--
 But fien' a hair care I.

When comin' hame on Sunday last
Upon the road, as I cam' past
Ye snufft an' gae your head a cast—
 But trouth I caretna by.

I doubt na lass, but ye may think
Because ye hae the name o' clink
That ye can please me at a wink
 Whene'er ye like to try.

But sorrow tak' him that's sae mean
Altho' his pouch o' coin were clean
That follows ony saucy quean
 That looks sae proud and high.

Altho' a lad were e'er sae smart
If that he want the yellow dirt
Ye'll cast your head anither airt
 An' answer him fu' dry.

But if he hae the name o' gear
Ye'll fasten till him like a breer
Tho' hardly he for sense or lear
 Be better than the ky.

But Tibby lass tak' my advice
Your Father's gear mak's you sae nice
The deil a ane wad speir your price
  Were ye as poor as I.

There lives a lass beside yon park
I'd rather hae her in her sark
Than you wi' a' your thousand mark
  That gars you look sae high.

An' Tibby I hae seen the day
Ye wadna been sae shy
An' for laik o' gear ye lightly me !—
  But fien a hair care I.

Sept.   SONG.

Tune.—Black Joke.

My girl she's airy, she's buxom and gay ;
Her breath is as sweet as the blossoms in May ;
  A touch of her lips it ravishes quite.
She's always good natur'd good humor'd and free ;
She dances, she glances, she smiles upon me
  I never am happy when out of her sight.
Her slender neck, her handsome waist,
Her hair well curled, her stays well lac'd,
Her taper white leg with
For her*
  And O for the joys of a long winter night.

    * Here the manuscript is defective.

JOHN BARLEYCORN—A SONG TO ITS OWN TUNE.

I once heard the old song, that goes by this name, sung, and being very fond of it, and remembering only two or three verses of it, viz., the 1st, 2d and 3d, with some scraps which I have interwoven here and there in the following piece:—

1785—June.

1

There was three kings into the East,
Three kings both great and high;
And they have sworn a solemn oath
That John Barleycorn should die.

2.

They've ta'en a plough and plough'd him down,
Put clods upon his head;
And they have sworn a solemn oath
That John Barleycorn was dead.

3.

But the spring time it came on,
And showers began to fall,
John Barleycorn got up again
And sore surpriz'd them all.

4.

The summer it came on,
And he grew thick and strong,

His head well arm'd with pointed spears
That no one should him wrong.

5.

The autumn it came on,
And he grew wan and pale;
His bending joints and drooping head
Show'd he began to fail.

6.

His color sickened more and more;
He faded into age;
And then his enemies began
To show their deadly rage.

7.

They took a hook was long and sharp
And cut him down at knee;
They ty'd him fast upon a cart
Like a rogue for forgery.

8.

They laid him down upon his back
And cudgel'd him full sore;
They hung him up before the storm
And turn'd him o'er and o'er.

9.

They filled up a darksome pit
With water to the brim

They've heaved in John Barleycorn
There let him sink or swin.

10.

They've thrown him out upon the floor
To work him farther woe;
And still as signs of life appear'd
They toss'd him to and fro.

11.

They wasted o'er a scorching flame
The marrow of his bones;
But the Miller used him worst of all
For he crush'd him between two stones.

12.

And they have ta'en his very heart's blood
And drank it round and round,
And still the more and more they drank
Their joy did more abound.

13.

John Barleycorn was a hero bold
Of noble enterprize,
For if you do but taste his blood
'Twill make your courage rise.

14.

'Twill make a man forget his woe,
And heighten all his joy;

'Twill make the widow's heart to sing
Tho' the tear were in her eye.

15.

Then let us toast John Barleycorn
Each man a glass in hand,
And may his great posterity
Ne'er fail in old Scotland.

FINIS.

June.—THE DEATH, AND DYIN' WORDS O' POOR MALIE
—MY AIN PET EWE—AN UNCO MOURNFU' TALE.

As Mailie and her lambs the gither
Were a'e day nibblin' on the tether,
Upon her cloot she coost a hitch
And o'er she warstled in the ditch.
There groanin', dyin' she did lye
When Hughoc he cam' doitin' by.
Wi' glowrin' een and lifted hands
Poor Hughoc like a statue stands ;
He saw her days were near hand ended,
But waes my heart, he couldna mend it ;
He gapit wide, but naething spak ;
At length poor Mailie silence brak.
O thou wha's lamentable face
Appears to mourn my woefu' case,

My dying words attentive hear
And bear them to my master dear.
Tell him, if e'er again he keep
As muckle gear as buy a sheep ;
O bid him never tye them mair
Wi' wicked strings o' hemp or hair ;
But caw them out to park or hill,
And let them wander at their will ;
So may his flock increase and grow
To score o' lambs and packs of woo'.
Tell him he was a master kind,
And ay was gude to me and mine ;
And now my dyin' charge I gie him,
My helpless lambs, I trust them wi' him.
O bid him save their harmless lives
Frae dogs, and tods, and butcher's knives ;
But gie them gude het milk their fill
Till they be fit to fen themsel' ;
And tent them duly e'en and morn
Wi' tates o' hay, and ripps o' corn.
O may they never learn the gaits
Of ither vile unrestfu' pets,
To slink thro' slaps, and reave and steal
At stacks o' pease, or stocks o' kail :
So may they, like their auld forbears,
For mony a year come thro' the shears,
So wives 'll gie them bits o' bread
And bairns greet for them when they're dead.

My poor toop lamb, my sinn and heir,
O bid him breed him up wi' care :
And if he live to be a beast
To put some havins in his breast.
And warn him ay at ridin' time
To stay content wi' ewes at hame,
And no to rin and wear his cloots
Like ither menseless, graceless brutes ;

And neist my ewie, silly thing,
Gude keep thee frae a tether string.
O may thou ne'er forgather up
Wi' ony blastit moorlan' tipp ;
But ay keep mind to moop and mell
Wi' sheep o' credit like thysel'.
And now my bairns, wi' my last breath
I li'e my blessin' wi' you baith :
And when ye ever mind your mither
Mind to be kind to ane anither.

Now honest Hughoc, dinna fail
To tell my master a' my tale ;
And bid him burn this cursed tether,
And for thy pains thou's get my blether.

This said, poor Mailie turn'd her head,
And clos'd her een amang the dead.

FINIS.

c

June.—A LETTER SENT TO JOHN LAPRAIK, NEAR MUIRKIRK, A TRUE GENUINE SCOTTISH BARD.

April 1st, 1785.

While breers and woodbines buding green,
And paitricks scraichin' loud at e'en,
And mornin' poosie whiddin' seen
      Inspire my muse,
This freedom in an unknown frien'
      I pray excuse.

On Fasten-e'en we had a rockin',
To ca' the crack and weave our stockin',
And there was meikle fun and jokin'
      Ye need na doubt ;
At length we had a hearty yokin'
      At sang about.

There was ae sang amang the rest
Aboon them a' it pleas'd me best
That some kind husband had addrest
      To some sweet wife
It touch'd the feelings o' the breast
      A' to the life.

I've scarce heard ought I pleas'd sae weel
The style sae tastie and genteel
Thought I, can this be Pope, or Steele,
      Or Beattie's wark

They tald me 'twas an odd kind chiel
      About Muirkirk
My heart was fidgin' fain to hear't
And sae about him a' I speirt
Then a' that kent him round declar't
      He was a devil
But had a frank and friendly heart
      Discreet and civil.
That set him to a pint of ale
And either douce or merry tale
Or rhymes and sangs he'd made himsel'
      Or witty catches
T'ween Inverness and Tiviotdale
      He had few matches.
Then up I gat, and swoor an aith
Though I should pawn my pleugh and graith
Or die a cadger pownie's death
      At some dyke back
A pint and gill I'd gi'e them baith
      To hear your crack.
But first and foremost I should tell
Amaist since ever I could spell
I've dealt in makin' rhymes mysel'
      Tho' rude and rough
But croonin' at a pleugh or fail
      Do weel enough.
I am nae Poet in a sense
But just a Rhymer like by chance

And hae to learnin' nae pretence
           Yet what the matter
Whene'er my Muse does on me glance
           I jingle at her.
Your Critic folk may cock their nose
And say how can you e'er propose,
You wha ken hardly verse by prose,
           To mak' a sang
But by your leaves my learned foes
           Ye're may-be wrang.
What's a' your jargon o' the schools
Your Latin names for horns and stools
If honest nature made you fools
           What sairs your grammars
Ye'd better ta'en up spades and shools
           Or knappin' hammers.
A set of silly senseless asses
Confuse their brains in colledge classes
They gang in stirks and come out asses
           Thus sae to speak
And then they think to climb Parnassus
           By dint o' Greek.
Gi'e me a'e spark o' nature's fire
That's a' the learnin' I desire.
Then tho' I drudge thro' dub and mire
           At pleugh or cart
My muse tho' hamely in attire
           May touch the heart.

O for a spunk o' Allan's glee
Or Ferguson the bauld and slee
Or tight Lapraik my friend to be
                If I can hit it
That would be lear enough for me
                If I could get it.
Now, Sir, if ye hae frien's enow
Tho' real frien's I b'lieve are few
Yet if your catalogue be fou,
                I'll no insist.
But if ye want a'e friend that's true
                I'm on your list.
I winna' blaw about mysel'
As ill I like my fauts to tell
But friends and folk that wish me well
                They sometimes roose me
Tho' I maun own as mony still
                As far abuse me.
Theres ae wee fau't they while's lay to me
1 like the lasses Gude forgi'e me
For mony a plack they wheedle frae me
                At dance or fair
May be some ither thing they gie me
                They weel can spare.
At Mauchline race, or Mauchline fair
I should be proud to meet you there
We'el gi'e ae night's discharge to care
                If we foregather

And hae a swap o' rhyming ware
          Wi' ane anither.
The four-gill chap we'll gar him clatter
And kirsen him wi' reekin' water
Syne we'se sit down and take our whitter
          To cheer our heart
And faith we'se be acquainted better
          Before we part.
Awa' ye selfish warldly race
Wha think that havins sense and grace
Even Love and Friendship should give place
          To Catch-the-plack
I dinna like to see your face
          Nor hear your crack
But ye whom social pleasure charms
Whose hearts true generous friendship warms
Who hold your beings on the terms
          " Each aid the others"
Come to my bowl—come to my arms
          My friends my brothers
But to conclude my lang Epistle
As my auld pen's worn to the gristle
Twa lines frae you wad gar me fistle
          Who am most fervent
While I can either sing or whistle,
          Your Friend and Servant,
Sic subscribitur   ———

On receiving an answer to the above I wrote the
following.

April 21st 1785.

While new ca't ky rowt at the stake
And pownies reek at pleugh or brake
This hour on e'enin's edge I take
      To own I'm debtor
To honest hearted auld Lapraik
      For his kind letter.
Forjesket sair wi' weary legs
Rattlin' the corn out owre the rigs
Or dealin' thro' amang the naigs
      Their ten hours bite
My dowie muse sair pleads and begs
      I would na write
The tapietless ramfeezl'd hissie
She's saft at best and something lazy
Quo she ye ken I've been sae bissie
      This month and mair
That trouth my head is grown right dissie
      And something sair.
Her dowf excuses pat me mad
Conscience says I ye thowless jad'
I'll write and that a hearty blaud
      This vera night
Sae dinna ye affront your trade
      But rhyme it right.

Shall bauld Lapraik the ace o' hearts
Tho' mankind were a pack o' cartes
Roose you sae weel for your deserts
   In terms sae friendly
Yet ye'll neglect to shaw your parts
   And thank him kindly
Sae I got paper in a blink
And in went stumpie in the ink
Says I before I sleep a wink
   I vow I'll close it
And if ye winna mak it clink
   By Jove I'll prose it.
But what my theme's to be, or whether
In rhyme or prose or baith the gither
Or some hotch-potch that's rightly neither
   Let time mak' proof
But I shall scribble doun some blether
   Just clean aff loof.
My worthy friend ne'er grudge and carp
Tho' fortune use you hard and sharp
Come kittle up your moorland harp
   Wi' gleesome touch
Ne'er mind how Fortune waft and warp
   She's but a b——
She's gien me mony a jirt and fleg
Sin' I could striddle o'er a rig
But by the l——d tho' I should beg
   Wi' lyart pow

I'll laugh, and sing, and shake my leg
        As lang's I dow.
Do ye envy the city Gent
Behint a kist to lie and sklent
Or purse-proud, big wi' cent per cent
        And muckle wame
In some bit Brugh to represent
        A Bailie's name.
Or is't the lordly feudal Thane
Wi' ruffl'd sark and glancin cane
Wha thinks himself nae sheep-shank bane
        But lordly stalks
While caps and bonnets aff are ta'en
        As by he walks.
May He wha gies us each good gift
Gie me o' wit and sense a lift
Then tho' he turn me out adrift,
        Thro Scotland wide
Wi' cits and lairds I wad na shift
        In a' their pride.
Were this the charter of our state
" On pain of Hell be rich and great "
Damnation then would be our fate
        Beyond remead
But thanks to Heaven that's no the gate
        We learn our creed.
For thus the royal mandate ran
Since first the Human-race began

"The social, friendly, honest man
              Whate'er he be,
'Tis he fulfils Great Nature's plan,
              And none but He."
O mandate, glorious and divine!
The followers o' the ragged Nine,
Poor honest devils, yet may shine
              In glorious light,
While sordid sons o' Mamon's line
              Are dark as night.
Tho' here they grunt, and scrape and growl,
Their silly nivefow o' a soul
May in some future carcase howl,
              The forest's fright;
Or in a day-detesting owl
              May shun the light.
Lapraik and Burness then may rise
And reach their native, kindred skies,
And sing their pleasures hopes and joys
              In some mild sphere
Still closer knit in Friendship's ties
              Each passing year.

August.   A SONG.

Tune.—Peggy Bawn.

When chill November's surly blast
Made fields and forests bare,

One evening as I wandered forth
Along the banks of Ayr;
I spi'd a man whose aged step
Seem'd weary worn with care
His face was furrow'd o'er with years
And hoary was his hair.

" Young Stranger whither wanderest thou,"
Began the rev'rend sage;
Does thirst of wealth thy step constrain,
Or youthful pleasure's rage:
Or hap'ly prest by cares and woes
Too soon thou hast began
To wander forth with me to mourn
The miseries of Man.

Yon sun that hangs o'er Carrick moors
That spreads so far and wide;
Where hundreds labor to support
The lordly Cassilis pride:
I've seen yon weary winter sun
Twice forty times return.
And every time has added proofs
That man was made to mourn.

O man! while in thy early years
How prodigal of time;
Mispending all those precious hours
Thy glorious youthful prime:

Alternate follies take the sway,
Licentious passions burn,
Which tenfold force give Nature's law
That, man was made to mourn.

Look not alone on youthful prime,
Or manhood's active might ;
Man then is useful to his kind,
Supported is his right :
But see him " on the edge of days "
With cares and labors worn,
Then Age and Want—O ill matched Pair !
Show man was made to mourn,

A few seem favorites of Fate
In Fortune's lap carest ;
Yet think not all the rich and great
Are likewise truly blest :
But O what crouds in ev'ry land
To wants and sorrows born,
Thro weary life this lesson learn
That man was made to mourn !

Many the ills that Nature's hand
Has woven with our frame :
More pointed still we make ourselves
Regret, remorse, and shame :
And Man, whose heaven-erected face
The smiles of love adorn,

Man's inhumanity to man
Makes countless thousands mourn.

See yonder poor o'erlabor'd wight
So abject, mean and vile ;
Who begs a brother of the earth
To give him leave to toil :
And see his lordly fellow-worm
The poor petition spurn,
Unmindful tho a weeping wife,
And helpless children mourn.

If I am doom'd yon Lordling slave,
By Nature's hand design'd,
Why was an independent wish
E'er planted in my mind ;
If not, why am I subject to
His cruelty or scorn
Or why has man the will and power
To make his fellow mourn.

Yet let not this too much, my son,
Disturb thy youthful breast ;
This partial view of Humankind
Is surely not the last ;
The poor, oppressed, honest heart
Had surely ne'er been born
Had there not been some recompence
To comfort those that mourn.

O Death ! the poor man's dearest friend,
The kindest and the best !
Welcome the hour my aged limbs
Are laid with thee at rest !
The Great, the Wealthy fear thy blow
From pomps, and pleasures torn ;
But oh ! a blest relief for those
That, weary-laden, mourn.

Aug.—However I am pleased with the works of our
Scotch Poets, particularly the excellent Ramsay, and the
still more excellent Ferguson, yet I am hurt to see other
places of Scotland, their towns, rivers, woods, haughs,
&c., immortalized in such celebrated performances,
whilst my dear native country, the ancient Bailieries of
Carrick, Kyle, and Cunningham, famous both in ancient
and modern times for a gallant and warlike race of in-
habitants, a country where civil, and particularly religious
Liberty have ever found their first support, and their
last asylum ; a country, the birthplace of many famous
Philosophers, Soldiers, and Statesmen, and the scene of a
great many important events recorded in Scottish History,
particularly a great many of the actions of the Glorious
Wallace, the Saviour of his country: Yet, we have never
had one Scotch Poet of any eminence, to make the fertile
banks of Irvine, the romantic woodlands and sequestered
scenes on Aire, and the heathy mountainous source, and
winding sweep of Doon, emulate Tay, Forth, Ettrick

Tweed, &c., this is a complaint I would gladly remedy, but Alas! I am far unequal to the task both in native genius and education. Obscure I am, and obscure I must be, though no young Poet, nor young Soldier's heart ever beat more fondly for fame than mine.

And if there is no other scene of Being
Where my insatiate wish may have its fill;
This something at my heart that heaves for room,
My best, my dearest part, was made in vain.

Aug.   A FRAGMENT.

Tune—I had a horse and I had nae mair.

When first I came to Stewart Kyle
My mind it was nae steady,
Where e'er I gaed, where e'er I rade,
A mistress still I had ay:
But when I came roun' by Mauchlin town,
Not dreadin' any body,
My heart was caught before I thought
And by a Mauchline Lady.

HAR'STE.—A FRAGMENT.

Tune—Foregoing,

Now breezy win's and slaughtering guns
Bring Autumn's pleasant weather,

And the muircock springs on whirring wings
Amang the blooming heather.
Now waving crops, with yellow tops,
Delight the weary Farmer,
An' the moon shines bright when I rove at night.
To muse on *

Sept.—There is a certain irregularity in the Old Scotch Songs, a redundancy of syllables with respect to that exactness of accent and measure that the English Poetry requires, but which glides in, most melodiously with the respective tunes to which they are set. For instance, the fine old song of "The Mill Mill O," to give it a plain prosaic reading, it halts prodigiously out of measure; on the other hand, the song set to the same tune in Bremner's collection of Scotch Songs which begins "To Fanny fair could I impart," &c., it is most exact measure, and yet, let them be both sung before a real Critic, one above the biasses of prejudice, but a thorough Judge of Nature, how flat and spiritless will the last appear, how trite, and lamely methodical, compared with the wild-warbling cadence, the heart-moving melody of the first. This particularly is the case with all those airs which end with a hypermetrical syllable. There is a degree of wild irregularity in many of the compositions and fragments which are daily sung to them by my compeers,

* The two closing words of the piece are in cypher.

the common people—a certain happy arrangement of
Old Scotch syllables, and yet, very frequently, nothing,
not even *like* rhyme, or sameness of jingle at the ends of
the lines. This has made me sometimes imagine that
perhaps, it might be possible for a Scotch Poet, with a
nice, judicious ear, to set compositions to many of our
most favorite airs, particularly that class of them mentioned above, independent of rhyme altogether. There
is a noble sublimity, a heart-melting tenderness in some
of these ancient fragments, which show them to be the
work of a masterly hand, and it has often given me
many a heartake to reflect that such glorious old Bards
—Bards, who, very probably, owed all their talents to
native genius yet have described the exploits of Heroes,
the pangs of Disappointment, and the meltings of Love
with such fine strokes of Nature, and, O mortifying to a
Bard's vanity their very names are " buried 'mongst the
wreck of things which were." O ye illustrious names unknown! the last the meanest of the Muses train, one who
tho' far far inferiour to your flights, yet eyes your path,
and with trembling wing would sometimes soar after you
A poor rustic Bard unknown, pays this sympathetic pang
to your memory !

O ye illustrious names unknown! who could feel
so strongly and describe so well! the last, the meanest
of the Muses train—one who, though far inferiour
to your flights, yet eyes your path, and with trem-

D

bling wing would sometimes soar after you—a poor, Rustic Bard unknown, pays this sympathetic pang to your memory! Some of you tell us, with all the charms of verse, that you have been unfortunate in the world, unfortunate in love; he too, has felt all the unfitness of a Poetic heart for the struggle of a busy, bad world; he has felt the loss of his little fortune, the loss of friends, and worse than all, the loss of the woman he adored! Like you, all his consolation was his Muse. She taught him in rustic measures to complain—Happy, could he have done it with your strength of imagination, and flow of verse! May the turf rest lightly on your bones! And may you now enjoy that solace and rest which this world rarely gives to the heart tuned to all the feelings of Poesy and Love!

Sept.—The following fragment is done, something in imitation of the manner of a noble old Scottish piece called M'Millan's Peggy, and sings to the tune of Galla water. My Montgomeries Peggy was my Deity for six, or eight months. She had been bred, tho' as the world says, without any just pretence for it, in a style of life rather elegant. But as Vanburgh says in one of his comedies, my " dam'd star found me out " there too, for though I began the affair, merely in a gaité de coeur, or to tell the truth, what would scarcely be believed, a vanity of showing my parts in Courtship, particularly my abilities at a Billet doux, which I always piqu'd myself upon, made me lay siege to her; and when, as I always do in my foolish gallantries, I had battered myself into a very warm affection for her, she told me, one day in a flag of truce, that her fortress had been for some time before the rightful property of another; but with the greatest friendship and politeness, she offered me every alliance, except actual possession. I found out afterwards, that what she told me of a pre-engagement was really true; but it cost some heart achs to get rid of the affair. I have even tryed to imitate in this extempore thing, that irregularity in the rhyme, which, when judiciously done, has such a fine effect on the ear.

FRAGMENT.

Tune—Galla Water.

Altho' my bed were in yon muir,
Amang the heather, in my plaidie,
Yet happy happy would I be
Had I my dear Montgomerie's Peggy.

When o'er the hill beat surly storms,
And winter nights were dark and rainy;
I'd seek some dell, and in my arms
I'd shelter dear Montgomerie's Peggy.

Were I a Baron proud and high,
And horse and servants waiting ready,
Then a' 'twad gie o' joy to me,
The shairin't with Montgomerie's Peggy.

Sept.—Another Fragment in imitation of an old Scotch Song, well known among the Country ingle sides. I cannot tell the name, neither of the Song nor the Tune but they are in fine unison with one another. By the way, these old Scottish airs are so nobly sentimental that when one would compose to them; to south the tune, as our Scotch phrase is, over and over, is the readiest way to catch the inspiration and raise the Bard into that glorious enthusiasm so strongly characteristic of our old Scotch poetry. I shall here set down one verse of the piece mentioned above, both to mark the song and tune I mean, and likewise as a debt I owe to the Author, as the repeating of that verse has lighted up my flame a thousand times. Alluding to the misfortunes he feelingly laments before this verse :—

> " When clouds in skies do come together
> " To hide the brightness of the sun,
> " There will surely be some pleasant weather
> " When a' thir storms are spent and gone."

> Though fickle Fortune has deceiv'd me,
> She promis'd fair and perform'd but ill ;
> Of mistress, friends, and wealth bereav'd me,
> Yet I bear a heart shall support me still.

> I'll act with prudence as far's I'm able
> But if success I must never find,

Then come misfortune, I bid thee welcome,
I'll meet thee with an undaunted mind.

The above was an extempore under the pressure of a heavy train of misfortunes, which indeed, threatened to undo me altogether. It was just at the close of that dreadful period mentioned page 8th; and though the weather has brightened up a little with me, yet there has always been since, a "tempest brewing round me in the grim sky" of futurity, which I pretty plainly see will, some time or other, perhaps ere long overwhelm me, and drive me into some doleful dell to pine in solitary, squalid wretchedness. However, as I hope my poor, country Muse, who, all rustic, awkward, and unpolished as she is, has more charms for me than any other of the pleasures of life beside—as I hope she will not then desert me, I may, even then, learn to be, if not happy, at least easy, and south a sang to sooth my misery. 'Twas at the same time I set about composing an air in the old Scotch style. I am not musical scholar enough to prick down my tune properly, so it can never see the light, and perhaps 'tis no great matter, but the following were the verses I composed to suit it.

O raging Fortune's withering blast
Has laid my leaf full low ! O

> O raging Fortune's withering blast
> Has laid my leaf full low ! O
> My stem was fair, my bud was green
> My blossom sweet did blow ; O
> The dew fell fresh, the sun rose mild,
> And made my branches grow ; O
> But luckless Fortune's northern storms
> Laid a' my blossoms low, O
> But luckless Fortune's northern storms
> Laid a' my blossoms low, O !

The tune consisted of three parts, so that the above verses just went through the whole air.

Oct. '85. If ever any young man, on the vestibule of the world, chance to throw his eye over these pages, let him pay a warm attention to the following observations; as I assure him they are the fruit of a poor devil's dear bought experience. I have, literally like that great poet and great gallant, and by consequence, that great fool, Solomon,—" turned my eyes to behold madness and folly,"—nay I have, with all the ardor of a lively, fanciful, and whimsical imagination, accompanied with a warm, feeling, poetic heart, shaken hands with their intoxicating friendship. In the first place, let my Pupil, as he tenders his own peace, keep up a regular, warm intercourse with the Deity.